G. Schirmer's Editions
of
Oratorios and Cantatas

The Seven Last Words
of Christ

A *Sacred* Cantata

For Soli, Chorus and Orchestra

The Music

by

THÉODORE DUBOIS

Ed. 186

A complete ORGAN SCORE, including all choral and
solo passages, by Norris L. Stevens is published.

G. SCHIRMER, Inc.

DISTRIBUTED BY

HAL•LEONARD®
CORPORATION
7777 W. BLUEMOUND RD. P.O. BOX 13819 MILWAUKEE, WI 53213

INDEX.

The Seven last Words of Christ.

Introduction.

Soprano Solo.

English adaptation by
Dr. Theo. Baker

THEODORE DUBOIS.

O vos omnes qui transitis per viam, atten - dite, et videte si est dolor sicut dolor meus._ Posuit me Dominus desolatam, totâ die mœ - rore confectam; no vocetis me Nœmi, sed vo - cate me Mara.

O all ye who travel upon the highway, heark - en to me, and behold me: was e'er sorrow like unto my sorrow? For the Lord Almighty hath dealt bitterly with me. Call me now no more Naomi, from to-day call me Mara.

14418 ×

4

Soprano Solo. *mf molto espressivo*

O vos om - nes qui tran-si-tis per
O all ye — who trav-el up-on the

vi - am, o vos om - nes qui tran-si-tis per vi - am,
high - way, O all ye — who trav-el up-on the high-way,

at - ten - di - te, et vi-de - te
heark - en to me, and be-hold me,

si est do - lor si-cut do-lor me - - us.
was e'er sor - row like un-to my sor - - row?

Po - su-it me Do-mi-nus de-so-la -
For the Lord Al - might-y, the Al - might -

tam, .to - tâ di - e moe-ro - re con - fec - tam;
y hath dealt bit-ter-ly, hath dealt bit-ter - ly with me;

ne vo-ce-tis me No - e - mi, sed vo-ca -
Call me now no more Na - o - mi, from to-day

8

First Word.
Baritone and Tenor Soli, with Chorus.

Pater, dimitte illis, non enim sciunt, quid faciunt.

Et dicebant omnes: Reus est mortis; tolle, tolle, crucifige eum. Sanguis ejus super nos et super filios nostros!

Crucifixerunt Jesum et latrones, unum a dextris et alterum a sinistris.

Father, forgive them, for they know not what they do.

And the people clamor'd: He is death-guilty; take him, take him, let us crucify him! Be his blood on us, and on our children!

Then they did crucify Jesus, and the two thieves, one at His right hand, the other at His left hand.

10

14418

et la - tro - nes,_____ u -
and the two thieves, _____ one _____

_ff_ SOPR.I.
tol - le!
take him!

_ff_ SOPR.II.
tol - le!
take him!

'Celli & D. B.
_mf_ _sost._
_p_ 'Celli & D.B.
Ped. Timp.

num a dex - tris et al - te - rum a si -
at His right ____ hand, the oth - er at His

nis - - tris. _p_ Cru - ci - fi -
left ____ hand; Then they did

Tromb.
_f_
Timp.
_p_
_f_
Ped. Ped.

Re - us est____ mor - tis; tol - le, tol - le,
he is death - guilt - y, take him, take him,

Re - us est mor - tis; tol - le, tol - le.
he is death - guilt - y, take him, take him,

Re - us est mor - tis; tol - le, tol - le,
he is death - guilt - y, take him, take him,

Re - us est mor - tis; tol - le, tol - le,
he is death - guilt - y, take him, take him,

Ped. ※ Ped. ※ Ped. ※ Ped. ※ Ped.

Baritone Solo. **Andante. 1º moto.**

Pa - ter, Pa - ter,
Fa - ther, Fa - ther,

tol - le!
take him!

tol - le!
take____ him!

tol - le!
take____ him!

tol - le!
take him!

Andante. 1º moto.
Harp.
mf

Second Word.
Duet for Tenor and Baritone, with Chorus.

Hodie mecum eris in Paradiso, amen, a-
men, dico tibi.

Domine, memento mei cum veneris in re-
gnum tuum.

Verily, thou shalt be in Paradise to-day
with me. Amen, so I tell thee.

Hear me, O Lord, and remember me, when
Thou comest into Thy kingdom.

28

11418

simile.

32

Third Word.

Soli for Soprano, Tenor, Baritone, with Chorus.

Mulier, ecce filius tuus.

Stabat Mater dolorosa
Juxta Crucem lacrymosa,
  Dum pendebat Filius.

Quis est homo, qui non fleret,
Christi Matrem si videret
  In tanto supplicio?

See, O woman! here behold thy Son beloved.

See yon mother, bow'd in anguish,
Who beside the cross doth languish,
  Where on high her son is borne;

Is there mortal, who not feeleth
To behold her where she kneeleth,
  So woeful, and all forlorn?

36

14418

Fourth Word.
Baritone Solo.

Deus meus, ut quid dereliquisti me?

Omnes amici mei dereliquerunt me; prævaluerunt insidiantes mihi; tradidit me quem diligebam.

Vinea mea electa, ego te plantavi; quomodo conversa es in amaratudine ut me crucifigeres?

God, my Father, why hast Thou forsaken me?

All those who were my friends, all have now forsaken me, and they that hate me do now prevail against me; and he whom I have cherished, he hath betray'd me.

Even the vine that I have chosen, and that I have planted: wherefore art thou now so strangely turned into bitterness, that I by thee am crucified?

44

14418

le - - cta, e - go te plan - ta - vi;
cho - - sen, and that I have plant - ed:

quo - mo - do con - ver - sa es in a - ma - ri
where - fore art thou now so strangely turn'd in - to

tu - di - ne ut cru - ci - fi - ge - res____ me?
bit - ter - ness, that I by thee am cru - ci - fied?

ut me cru - ci - fi
that I by thee am

Fifth Word.

Chorus, and Soli for Tenor and Baritone.

Sitio!

Judæi prætereuntes blasphemabant eum, moventes capita sua et dicentes:Vah!qui destruis templum Dei, si tu es Christus, Filius Dei, descende nunc de cruce, ut videamus et credamus tibi.—Si tu es rex Judeorum, salvum te fac.

I am athirst!

And the Jews then passing by him, all did rail upon him, and wagging their heads at him, they said unto him:

Ah! Thou wouldst fain destroy the temple; if thou be Jesus, Son of the Father, now from the cross descend thou, that we behold it, and believe on thee when we behold it. If thou art king over Israel, save thyself, then!

14418

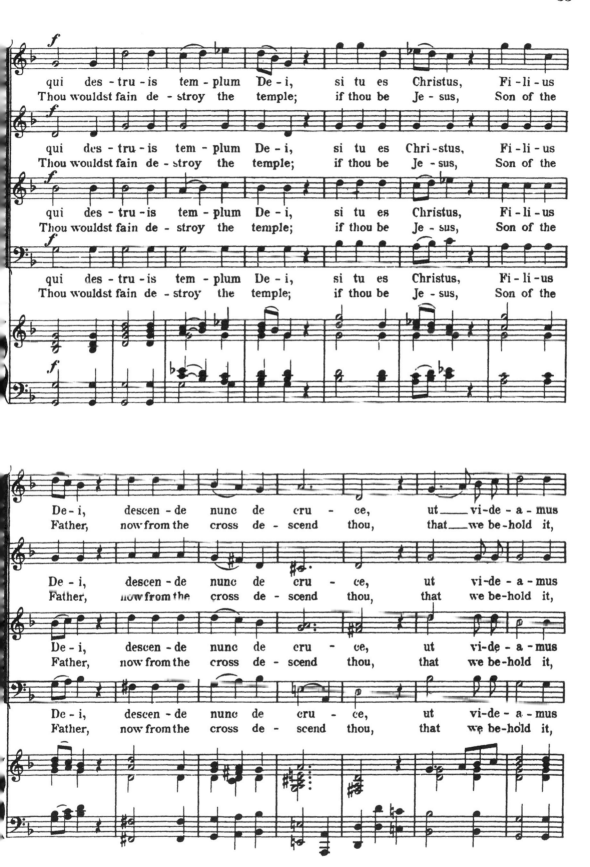

qui des-tru-is tem-plum De-i, si tu es Christus, Fi-li-us
Thou wouldst fain de-stroy the temple; if thou be Je-sus, Son of the

qui des-tru-is tem-plum De-i, si tu es Chri-stus, Fi-li-us
Thou wouldst fain de-stroy the temple; if thou be Je-sus, Son of the

qui des-tru-is tem-plum De-i, si tu es Christus, Fi-li-us
Thou wouldst fain de-stroy the temple; if thou be Je-sus, Son of the

qui des-tru-is tem-plum De-i, si tu es Christus, Fi-li-us
Thou wouldst fain de-stroy the temple; if thou be Je-sus, Son of the

De-i, descen-de nunc de cru-ce, ut___ vi-de-a-mus
Father, now from the cross de-scend thou, that___ we be-hold it,

De-i, descen-de nunc de cru-ce, ut vi-de-a-mus
Father, now from the cross de-scend thou, that we be-hold it,

De-i, descen-de nunc de cru-ce, ut vi-de-a-mus
Father, now from the cross de-scend thou, that we be-hold it,

De-i, descen-de nunc de cru-ce, ut vi-de-a-mus
Father, now from the cross de-scend thou, that we be-hold it,

56

14418

Sixth Word.
Tenor Solo, and Chorus.

Pater, in manus tuas commendo spiritum meum.
Pater meus es tu, Deus meus, susceptor salutis meae.
In manus tuas commendo spiritum meum.

Father, into Thy hands I commend my soul.
For Thou art my God and my Father;
Thou art my Saviour.
Into Thy hands I commend my soul.

Seventh Word.
Solo for Soprano, Tenor and Baritone, with Chorus.

Et clamans Jesu voce magna dixit: *Consummatum est!*

Et inclinato capite, tradidit spiritum.

Erat autem fere hora sexta; obscuratus est sol, et tenebræ factæ sunt in universam terram; velum templi scissum est: omnis terra tremuit; petræ scissæ et monumenta aperta sunt.

Prayer.

Adoramus te, Christe. et benedicimus tibi.quia per sanctam Crucem tuam redemisti mundum.

And with a loud voice Jesus cried, exclaiming: *It is finished!*

And He did bow His head, and rendered up His spirit.

And it was about the sixth hour; and the sun was darkened, and darkness covered the earth, until about the ninth hour; and the veil of the temple was rent, and all the earth did quake; and the rocks were rent, and all the graves were opened wide.

Prayer.

Christ, we do all adore Thee, and we do praise Thee for ever; for on the holy cross hast thou the world from sin redeemed.

om - nis ter - ra tre - mu - it;
and all the earth did quake;

cresc. ed allarg. molto _ _ _ _ _

pe - træ scis - - - sæ et mo - nu -
and the rocks were rent, and all the

colla voce

cresc. ed allarg. molto _ _ _

Piccolo

Tamtam.

men - - ta a - per - ta sunt.
graves _ were o - pen'd wide.

Allegro molto. (♩ = 96.)

Piccolo

Str. and Piccolo

Timp.

Remark. It is by far most preferable to sing this Chorus with the great organ. The organ would then double the voices with very soft stops--*gamba* and *voix céleste*.